the little
book of
Women's
Wit

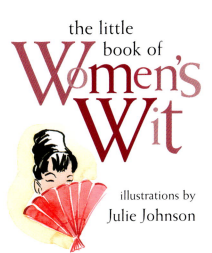

illustrations by

Julie Johnson

Lawrence Teacher Books
=== Philadelphia ===

Mechanicals produced by book soup publishing, inc.
Cover design by Maria Lewis and Susan Van Horn
Interior design by Susan Van Horn
Illustrations © 2000 by Julie Johnson
Quotes compiled by Melissa Lieberman
Edited by Erin Slonaker

ISBN 1-930408-01-3

10 9 8 7 6 5 4 3 2 1

Please support your local book or gift store.
However, if you cannot find this book there,
you may order it directly from the publisher.
Please add $1.50 for postage and handling.
Send check or money order to the address below.

Lawrence Teacher Books
2611 Bainbridge Street
Philadelphia, PA 19146

Contents

Introduction

The next best thing to being clever is being able to quote someone who is.

MARY PETTIBONE POOLE (B.1938)

The essence of wit cuts straight through to the essence of life, the unavoidable truths. And what makes women's wit unique is that it speaks, precisely and cleverly, to the heart of what womanhood is.

The feminine perspective has changed throughout the years, as the role of woman has changed. In our evolution from wives and home-makers to voters and equal rights activists to CEOs and VIPs, we have always had a special and singular point of view of the world at large, and "at small." Using our "wits," we can comment on life around us. Using wit to shine a surprising light on familiar topics such as motherhood or romance can get right to the heart of the reality of a woman's world, the highs and lows of our quest for success and fulfillment, and explain to the rest of the world how exciting and frustrating—and real— our realities, our everydays, can be.

Wit, with grace, joy, and poignance, gives us the perspective to step back, to look on in wonder, to laugh, and to embrace life. This little book can help us all to do just that.

Life as a Woman

Being powerful is like being a lady. If you have to tell people you are, you aren't.

MARGARET THATCHER,
BRITISH POLITICIAN (B. 1925)

I don't care what is written about me so long as it isn't true.

KATHARINE HEPBURN,
AMERICAN ACTOR (B. 1909)

LEAD ME NOT INTO
TEMPTATION; I CAN FIND
THE WAY MYSELF.

RITA MAE BROWN,
AMERICAN WRITER (B. 1944)

Sometimes I feel
like a figment of my
own imagination.

Lily Tomlin,
American comedian, actor (b. 1939)

A woman is like a tea bag—
only in hot water do you realize
how strong she is.

NANCY REAGAN,
AMERICAN FIRST LADY (B. 1923)

To err is human,
but it feels divine.

MAE WEST,
AMERICAN ACTOR (1893–1980)

I'VE NEVER UNDERSTOOD
WHY PEOPLE CONSIDER
YOUTH A TIME OF FREEDOM
AND JOY. IT'S PROBABLY
BECAUSE THEY HAVE
FORGOTTEN THEIR OWN.

MARGARET ATWOOD,
CANADIAN WRITER (B. 1939)

From birth to age eighteen, a girl needs good parents; from eighteen to thirty-five, she needs good looks; from thirty-five to fifty-five, she needs a good personality; and from fifty-five on, she needs cash.

SOPHIE TUCKER,
AMERICAN SINGER (1884–1966)

I base most of my fashion taste on what doesn't itch.

GILDA RADNER,
AMERICAN COMEDIAN, ACTOR
(1946–1989)

The really frightening thing about middle age is the knowledge that you'll grow out of it.

DORIS DAY,
AMERICAN ACTOR (B. 1924)

THE PROBLEM WITH BEAUTY
IS THAT IT'S LIKE BEING BORN
RICH AND GETTING
PROGRESSIVELY POORER.

JOAN COLLINS,
BRITISH ACTOR (B. 1933)

I'm not going to vacuum 'til Sears makes one you can ride on.

ROSEANNE BARR,
AMERICAN COMEDIAN, ACTOR (B. 1952)

I did not use paint.
I made myself
up morally.

ELEANORA DUSE,
ITALIAN ACTOR (1859–1924)

I STOPPED BELIEVING IN
SANTA CLAUS AT AN EARLY
AGE. MOTHER TOOK ME TO
SEE HIM IN A DEPARTMENT
STORE AND HE ASKED FOR
MY AUTOGRAPH.

SHIRLEY TEMPLE BLACK,
AMERICAN ACTOR, DIPLOMAT (B. 1928)

For a single woman, preparing for company means wiping the lipstick off the milk carton.

ELAYNE BOOSLER,
AMERICAN COMEDIAN (B. 1952)

Good girls go to heaven,
bad girls go everywhere.

HELEN GURLEY BROWN,
AMERICAN EDITOR (B. 1922)

Marriage
and
Family

The trouble with some women is they get all excited about nothing—and then they marry him.

CHER,
AMERICAN SINGER, ACTOR (B. 1946)

*Constant togetherness
is fine—but only for
Siamese twins.*

VICTORIA BILLINGS,
AMERICAN JOURNALIST (B. 1945)

BROUGHT UP TO RESPECT
THE CONVENTIONS, LOVE
HAD TO END IN MARRIAGE.
I'M AFRAID IT DID.

BETTE DAVIS,
AMERICAN ACTOR (1908–1989)

Marriage is the only thing that affords a woman the pleasure of company and the perfect sensation of solitude at the same time.

HELEN ROWLAND,
AMERICAN WRITER (1876–1950)

I'm an excellent housekeeper.
Every time I get a divorce,
I keep the house.

ZSA ZSA GABOR,
HUNGARIAN ACTOR (B. 1917)

My husband says the only thing domestic about me is that I was born in this country.

PHYLLIS DILLER,
AMERICAN COMEDIAN (B. 1917)

I LOVE BEING MARRIED.
IT'S SO GREAT TO FIND THAT
ONE SPECIAL PERSON YOU
WANT TO ANNOY FOR THE
REST OF YOUR LIFE.

RITA RUDNER,
AMERICAN COMEDIAN (B. 1956)

If love means never having to say you're sorry, then marriage means having to say everything twice.

ESTELLE GETTY,
AMERICAN ACTOR (B. 1924)

ANY INTELLIGENT WOMAN
WHO READS THE MARRIAGE
CONTRACT AND THEN
GOES INTO IT DESERVES ALL
THE CONSEQUENCES.

ISADORA DUNCAN,
AMERICAN DANCER (1878–1927)

A wedding invitation is a beautiful and formal notification of the desire to share a solemn and joyous occasion, sent by people who have been saying "Do we have to ask them?" to people whose first response is "How much do you think we have to spend on them?"

JUDITH "MISS MANNERS" MARTIN, AMERICAN ESSAYIST (B. 1938)

Children's talent to endure stems from their ignorance of alternatives.

MAYA ANGELOU,
AMERICAN WRITER (B. 1928)

1360 BC

An archaeologist is the best husband any woman can have; the older she gets, the more interested he is in her.

AGATHA CHRISTIE,
BRITISH WRITER (1890–1976)

We spend the first twelve months of our children's lives teaching them to walk and talk and the next twelve telling them to sit down and shut up.

PHYLLIS DILLER,
AMERICAN COMEDIAN (B. 1917)

The best way to keep children at home is to make the home atmosphere pleasant—and let the air out of their tires.

DOROTHY PARKER,
AMERICAN WRITER (1893–1967)

IT TAKES A WOMAN
TWENTY YEARS TO MAKE
A MAN OF HER SON, AND
ANOTHER WOMAN
TWENTY MINUTES TO
MAKE A FOOL OF HIM.

HELEN ROWLAND,
AMERICAN WRITER (1876–1950)

Never lend your car to anyone to whom you have given birth.

Erma Bombeck,
American humorist, essayist
(1927–1996)

Women and Men

*When a man gives
his opinion he's a man,
when a woman gives her
opinion she's a bitch.*

BETTE DAVIS,
AMERICAN ACTOR (1908–1989)

A man has to be
Joe McCarthy to be
called ruthless. All a
woman has to do is
put you on hold.

MARLO THOMAS,
AMERICAN ACTOR (B. 1938)

YOU SEE A LOT OF SMART
GUYS WITH DUMB WOMEN,
BUT YOU HARDLY EVER
SEE A SMART WOMAN WITH
A DUMB GUY.

ERICA JONG,
AMERICAN WRITER (B. 1942)

*Women want mediocre men,
and men are working to be
as mediocre as possible.*

MARGARET MEAD,
AMERICAN ANTHROPOLOGIST
(1901–1978)

Most women set out to try to change a man, and when they have changed him they don't like him.

MARLENE DIETRICH,
GERMAN ACTOR (1901–1992)

The only time a woman really succeeds in changing a man is when he is a baby.

NATALIE WOOD,
AMERICAN ACTOR (1938–1981)

Women have served all
these centuries as looking-glasses
possessing the magic and delicious
power of reflecting the figure of
a man at twice its natural size.

VIRGINIA WOOLF,
BRITISH WRITER (1882–1941)

A MAN IS DESIGNED TO WALK
THREE MILES IN THE RAIN TO
PHONE FOR HELP WHEN THE
CAR BREAKS DOWN—AND A
WOMAN IS DESIGNED TO SAY,
"YOU TOOK YOUR TIME" WHEN
HE COMES BACK DRIPPING WET.

VICTORIA WOOD,
BRITISH WRITER, COMEDIAN (B. 1953)

Whether women are better than men, I cannot say. But I can say that they are no worse.

GOLDA MEIR,
ISRAELI PRIME MINISTER (1898–1978)

I've been on so
many blind dates,
I should get a
free dog.

WENDY LIEBMAN,
AMERICAN COMEDIAN (B. 1961)

A woman without a man
is like a fish without a bicycle.

GLORIA STEINEM,
AMERICAN ACTIVIST, WRITER,
EDITOR (B. 1934)

IF YOU TEACH A MAN,
HE WILL BE TRAINED IN
ONE SKILL; IF YOU TEACH
A WOMAN, THE WHOLE
FAMILY WILL LEARN
WHAT SHE LEARNS.

RUBY MANIKAN,
20TH CENTURY INDIAN CHURCH LEADER

Men and women are
like right and left hands:
it doesn't make sense
not to use both.

JEANNETTE RANKIN,
AMERICAN CONGRESSWOMAN
(1880–1973)

Man invented language to satisfy his deep need to complain.

LILY TOMLIN,
AMERICAN COMEDIAN, ACTOR (B. 1939)

I DON'T MIND LIVING IN A
MAN'S WORLD, AS LONG AS I
GET TO BE A WOMAN IN IT.

MARILYN MONROE,
AMERICAN ACTOR (1926–1962)

Sometimes I wonder if men and women really suit each other. Perhaps they should live next door and just visit now and then.

KATHARINE HEPBURN,
AMERICAN ACTOR (B. 1909)

*Behind almost every
woman you've heard
of stands a man who
let her down.*

NAOMI BLIVEN,
AMERICAN WRITER (B. 1925)

There are men
I could spend
eternity with, but
not in this life.

KATHLEEN NORRIS,
AMERICAN WRITER (1880–1966)

Being Feminist

People call me a feminist whenever I express sentiments that distinguish me from a doormat or a prostitute.

I'm furious about the Women's Liberationists. They keep getting up on soapboxes and proclaiming that women are brighter than men. That's true, but it should be kept quiet or it ruins the whole racket.

ANITA LOOS,
AMERICAN WRITER (1893–1981)

I BECAME A FEMINIST AS
AN ALTERNATIVE TO
BECOMING A MASOCHIST.

SALLY KEMPTON,
AMERICAN WRITER (B. 1943)

Some of us are becoming the men we wanted to marry.

GLORIA STEINEM,
AMERICAN ACTIVIST, WRITER,
EDITOR (B. 1934)

I am not belittling the brave pioneer men, but the sunbonnet as well as the sombrero has helped to settle this glorious land of ours.

EDNA FERBER,
AMERICAN WRITER (1885–1968)

If the world were a logical place, men would ride side-saddle.

RITA MAE BROWN,
AMERICAN WRITER (B. 1944)

JUST BECAUSE EVERYTHING
IS DIFFERENT DOESN'T
MEAN THAT ANYTHING
HAS CHANGED.

IRENE PETER,
20TH CENTURY AMERICAN WRITER

Just because we're sisters under the skin doesn't mean we've got much in common.

Angela Carter,
British writer (1940–1992)

Tremendous amounts of talent are being lost to our society just because that talent wears a skirt.

SHIRLEY CHISHOLM,
AMERICAN CONGRESSWOMAN (B. 1924)

We have lived through the era when happiness was a warm puppy, and the era when happiness was a dry martini, and now we have come to the era when happiness is "knowing what your uterus looks like."

NORA EPHRON,
AMERICAN WRITER, DIRECTOR (B. 1941)

What It All Means

*Happiness is good health
and a bad memory.*

INGRID BERGMAN,
SWEDISH ACTOR (1915–1982)

Friendship is
mutual blackmail
elevated to the
level of love.

ROBIN MORGAN,
AMERICAN ACTIVIST, WRITER (B. 1941)

COURAGE IS THE PRICE
THAT LIFE EXACTS FOR
GRANTING PEACE.

AMELIA EARHART,
AMERICAN AVIATOR (1897–1937)

The worst part of success
is trying to find someone who
is happy for you.

BETTE MIDLER,
AMERICAN ACTOR, SINGER (B. 1945)

Jealousy is all the fun
you think they had.

ERICA JONG,
AMERICAN WRITER (B. 1942)

The trouble with the rat
race is that even if you win
you're still a rat.

LILY TOMLIN,
AMERICAN ACTOR (B. 1939)

Success is always something that you have to recover from.

MARSHA NORMAN,
AMERICAN PLAYWRIGHT (B. 1947)

The penalty of success is to be bored by people who used to snub you.

NANCY ASTOR,
BRITISH POLITICIAN (1879–1964)

Success is counted sweetest
By those who ne'er succeed.

EMILY DICKINSON,
AMERICAN POET (1830–1886)

REALITY IS SOMETHING
YOU RISE ABOVE.

LIZA MINNELLI,
AMERICAN ACTOR, SINGER (B. 1946)

Strength is the capacity to break a chocolate bar into four pieces with your bare hands—and then eat just one of the pieces.

JUDITH VIORST,
AMERICAN WRITER (B. 1931)

*Normal is in the eye
of the beholder.*

WHOOPI GOLDBERG,
AMERICAN ACTOR, COMEDIAN (B. 1949)

BEING AN OLD MAID
IS LIKE DEATH BY
DROWNING, A REALLY
DELIGHTFUL SENSATION
AFTER YOU CEASE
TO STRUGGLE.

Edna Ferber,
American writer (1887–1968)

Dancing is like bank robbery. It takes split-second timing.

TWYLA THARP, AMERICAN
DANCER, CHOREOGRAPHER (B. 1941)

The most radical revolutionary will become a conservative the day after the revolution.

HANNAH ARENDT,
AMERICAN HISTORIAN (1906–1975)

The opposite of
talking isn't listening.
The opposite of talking
is waiting.

FRAN LEBOWITZ,
AMERICAN WRITER (B. 1950)

Advice and Wisdom

ALL MY LIFE, I ALWAYS
WANTED TO BE SOMEBODY.
NOW I SEE THAT I SHOULD
HAVE BEEN MORE SPECIFIC.

JANE WAGNER,
AMERICAN WRITER (B. 1927)

Although the whole world is full of suffering, it is also full of the overcoming of it.

HELEN KELLER,
AMERICAN WRITER, EDUCATOR
(1880–1968)

Advice is what we ask for
when we already know the
answer but wish we didn't.

ERICA JONG,
AMERICAN WRITER (B. 1942)

*Where an opinion is general,
it is usually correct.*

JANE AUSTEN,
BRITISH WRITER (1775–1817)

NOTHING IS SO GOOD
AS IT SEEMS BEFOREHAND.

GEORGE ELIOT,
BRITISH WRITER (1819–1880)

When nothing is sure,
everything is possible.

Margaret Drabble,
British writer (b. 1939)

The real reason
for comedy is to
hide the pain.

WENDY WASSERSTEIN,
AMERICAN PLAYWRIGHT (B. 1950)

Comedy is tragedy that happens to other people.

ANGELA CARTER,
BRITISH WRITER (1940–1992)

Everything is so
dangerous that nothing
is really very frightening.

GERTRUDE STEIN,
AMERICAN WRITER (1874–1946)

YOU DON'T HAVE
TO FIGHT IN A WAR TO
LOVE PEACE.

GERALDINE FERRARO,
AMERICAN POLITICIAN (B. 1935)

The way I see it, if you want the rainbow, you gotta put up with the rain.

DOLLY PARTON,
AMERICAN SINGER, ACTOR (B. 1946)

*You can no more
win a war than win
an earthquake.*

JEANNETTE RANKIN,
AMERICAN CONGRESSWOMAN
(1880–1973)

I ALWAYS HAVE A
QUOTATION FOR
EVERYTHING—IT SAVES
ORIGINAL THINKING.

DOROTHY L. SAYERS,
BRITISH WRITER (1893–1957)

Love thy neighbor
as thyself,
but choose your
neighborhood.

LOUISE BEAL,
AMERICAN WRITER (1844–1910)

People change
and forget to tell
each other.

LILLIAN HELLMAN,
AMERICAN PLAYWRIGHT (1905–1984)

God gives us our relatives; thank God we can choose our friends!

ETHEL WATTS MUMFORD,
AMERICAN WRITER (1878–1940)

TOO MANY COOKS MAY
SPOIL THE BROTH,
BUT IT ONLY TAKES ONE
TO BURN IT.

JULIA CHILD,
AMERICAN CHEF (B. 1912)

Food is an important part
of a balanced diet.

FRAN LEBOWITZ,
AMERICAN WRITER (B. 1950)

It takes two flints
to make a fire.

LOUISA MAY ALCOTT,
AMERICAN WRITER (1832–1888)

People who fight fire with fire usually end up with the ashes.

ABIGAIL VAN BUREN,
AMERICAN COLUMNIST (B. 1918)

MILLIONS LONG FOR
IMMORTALITY WHO DON'T
KNOW WHAT TO DO ON A
RAINY AFTERNOON.

SUSAN ERTZ,
AMERICAN WRITER (1894–1985)

Whoever said, "it's not whether you win or lose that counts," probably lost.

MARTINA NAVRATILOVA,
CZECH-BORN AMERICAN TENNIS
CHAMPION (B. 1956)

If you want a place in the sun, you've got to put up with a few blisters.

ABIGAIL VAN BUREN,
AMERICAN COLUMNIST (B. 1918)

Rose-colored glasses are
never made in bifocals.
Nobody wants to read the
fine print in dreams.

ANN LANDERS,
AMERICAN COLUMNIST (B. 1918)

See into
life—don't just
look at it.

ANNE BAXTER,
AMERICAN ACTRESS (1923–1987)